# Andrew's Animals

## About the Author

Andrew Dodd, MVB, MRCVS, MA, qualified as a vet in Dublin in 1989. He then moved to Buckinghamshire, where he worked with horses and small animals, and was a veterinary consultant for film and television productions at Pinewood Studios. This inspired him to take a Masters degree in film studies, which he received in 1993 from University College, Dublin, writing his thesis on the symbolic meanings of the dog and the cat in film. In 1994 he began presenting the hows and whys of animal behaviour to a wide audience on RTE's Pat Kenny Radio Show. As Pet Vet for Network 2's Den TV, he enjoys making everything from cheetahs to chickens accessible to children. He has a successful small animal practice in Dublin. *Andrew's Animals* is his first book.

# Andrew's Animals

## ANDREW DODD

POOLBEG

Published in 1995 by
Poolbeg Press Ltd
Knocksedan House,
123 Baldoyle Industrial Estate,
Dublin 13, Ireland

A catalogue record for this book is available from the British Library.

ISBN 1 85371 533 6

Illustrations by Graeme Keyes
Cover design by Poolbeg Group Services Ltd
Set by Poolbeg Group Services in Joanna 14/15
Printed by The Guernsey Press Ltd,
Vale, Guernsey, Channel Islands.

# ACKNOWLEDGEMENTS

I warmly thank:

Nicole Jussek – my editor – and everyone at Poolbeg
Dale Parry – my manager and advisor
Randal Faulkner and Anthony Gallagher at FEBO for all
their support
Alma Elvin the art director, who designed the *Andrew's
Animals* logo
All at The Helme Partnership especially Donald Helme
Graeme Keyes for his illustrations
The Pat Kenny Show RTE Radio 1
Stuart Krichevsky – my literary agent
Maria Blair for typing the manuscript
And a huge thank you to Marty Boroson – for everything

This book is dedicated to my parents,
Ruth and Vincent

# Contents

## Why *Andrew's Animals*?

Three years ago I realised that there was more to animals than what we were taught in veterinary school. I had learned how to treat sick domestic animals, but had not learned much about exotic animals, or the huge diversity of animal behaviour and culture. So, I collected information about other aspects of animal life. What I found out about animal behaviour I thought would strike people as quirky, funny, enchanting, cruel, and sometimes even shocking. It even puts some of our own "eccentric" behaviour into perspective. I began to talk all about this regularly on the Pat Kenny Radio Show. The response convinced me that many people love learning what the furry and the feathered are really doing out there.

# WHAT HAPPENS AT HATCHING?

**HATCHING** is the term used to describe emergence of a developed chick from its egg shell. Although it looks easy, this apparently simple event involves a lot of preparation, most of which is hidden from us.

By the time a chick hatches, its shell has been weakened through the loss of minerals depleted from it which are used in building the chick's skeleton. Baby birds don't peck their way out of the shell as we are often told. Just before hatching, they move around inside the shell, repositioning themselves so that the beak is near the air sac at the blunt or round end of the egg. This air sac is then burst and the baby bird or **EMBRYO** comes in contact with air for the first time and begins to breathe like hatched birds do. A hard bump on the tip of its beak is the only tool the chick has to use. Little jerks start, like backward headbanging, flicking the beak against the inside of the shell. A crack forms, followed by a tiny hole called a **PIPPING HOLE**. Inside the shell the chick now begins cheeping – if it hasn't already started. The beak is now visible to spectators watching the event. To make the hole bigger, the shell's occupant slowly rotates on its bottom in an anticlockwise fashion while still beating its beak against the inside of the shell. This causes more cracking of the shell. The whole shell cap eventually separates and the chick wriggles slowly out of the remaining lower half of the shell.

There are two kinds of hatchlings. Some, like baby chickens, hatch in quite a developed state. Covered in downy feathers, they come into the world with their eyes open and are able to run around as soon as they have left the shell behind. Baby chickens also have built-in food reserves which keep them going until they find their own food. Other hatchlings, like baby pigeons, are born without feathers or food reserves. Their eyes aren't open yet and they rely entirely on their parents for food and shelter.

Hatching is an exhausting process for any baby bird and they generally do it completely unaided. Even when parent birds are present to witness their offspring hatching they seldom help the chick out of its shell – hatching is the first fitness test in a baby bird's life.

# Why Do Bees Die After Stinging?

In truth, any bee given the choice would prefer to make honey than sting anyone. It will attack only as a last resort – partly because it will be the last act to which it resorts.

The bee seems to follow the old military maxim that "attack is the best method of defence" and will sting only to protect its colony or hive, or if trying to escape from some creature foolish enough to interfere with it. Unfortunately, this act of defence has "a sting in the tail" and turns out to be a once-in-a-lifetime action – resulting in the bee's death.

The reason the bee can sting only once is that the weapon – or stinger – is left behind in the victim after the bee has escaped; there can be no reloading procedure. The sting itself, which sits in the sting chamber like a bullet in a gun-barrel, is a straight, tapering tube with little barbs and blades at the tip and a poison sac at the base.

When threatened, the angry bee jabs its

victim with the stinger which enters the skin. Here it is drawn deeper into the flesh as poison is pumped through the tube. Having got its revenge the "hit-and-run" bee decides to make good its escape. However, the stinger, now firmly embedded in the victim, is ripped out of the bee's body as it flies off, leaving the poison sacs behind still pumping. The amount of venom injected is actually quite small; only about one quarter of a milligram.

The sting of the Queen Bee is different. Her stinger doesn't break off and is used only for stinging rival Queens. When fighting, these majestic bees just jab their stings repeatedly into each other, withdrawing the stinger unharmed each time.

While a bee sting may cause discomfort to its human victim, it is the stinger, not the stung, who pays the ultimate price for this briefest of encounters. This aggressive act causes such massive internal damage due to the rupturing of delicate tissues by which the sting was attached that, within a short time, the bee is dead.

# Do Sloths Do Everything Slowly?

There are two well-known types of sloth: the two-toed sloth and the three-toed sloth. The main physical difference between them is, well, fairly obvious.

Sloths basically invented slow motion. From the day they are born to the day they die they are in low gear. Sloths feed on the leaves of the trees on which they themselves hang. They don't derive much nourishment or energy from this food, but hey, they don't need much because they do so very little!

Because they get so little energy from their food, sloths have to do everything possible to conserve their stores. A lot of energy is used up just keeping warm. Sloths are warm-blooded animals and to help minimise heat loss during cold periods they are covered in a very dense fur which is prone to moth infestation.

As the arms of sloths are much longer than their legs, they move sluggishly and look ungainly. They are not able to walk on all fours and, when on the ground, must pull

"I'M GOING TO TAKE FORTY THOUSAND WINKS..."

themselves along with their forelimbs. One would need to be very slow indeed to be slower than a sloth. Being dawdlers by nature they're prime targets for predators and, only able to move at about ten feet per minute, are hopeless at running away. A sloth will generally hang quite still in the tree where it lives. This total immobility, together with its long coat, helps disguise the sloth from predators. Its colour varies from season to season. When the weather is damp, the sloth takes on the greenish vegetable tinge of the algae. This changes to yellow when the weather becomes very dry or a drought occurs.

Sloths often live in and eat the leaves of trees which are poisonous. They are, however, capable of taking the poisons out and digesting the leaves . . . very slowly. One meal can take as much as a month to digest! Sloths defecate only once a week. Climbing down from its favourite branch the sloth will hang from a vine and scratch a hole in the ground where it deposits its dung.

Nothing ever seems to ruffle sloths and it is difficult to decipher how they feel. Their lethargic approach to life certainly makes you wonder why they bother!

# How Do Vampire Bats Feed?

Bats have huge appetites. Because of their big bare wing span they lose heat constantly. Frequent meals help replace this heat. Vampire bats feed on blood – fresh blood. Unlike lots of other bats, their eyesight is excellent. They wait until it is pitch dark before going in search of a juicy host and can easily sniff out a good meal while flying around. Luckily for us, they don't often go for the taste of human blood; cattle blood seems to be their favourite. Vampire bats seldom bite dogs because of the dog's ability to hear their high frequency sounds as they approach.

When the bats have located a herd of beefy blood banquets they fly in and land close by. A victim is chosen and the bat approaches it, walking on all fours. Unlike fictional human vampires, the vampire bat doesn't go for the jugular vein in the neck, preferring the shoulders or sides of the animal – any area that doesn't have much hair. Once the spot has been chosen, two front teeth, sharp as razor blades, swiftly bite through the skin and a V-shaped incision is made. The victim rarely reacts to the bite. If it does, the bat just flies off. When the bat taps into flowing blood it starts to feed.

Blood clots very quickly when it comes in contact with air. To prevent this from happening while the bat is feeding, a special ANTICOAGULANT in the vampire diner's saliva keeps the blood flowing. This type of vampire doesn't actually suck blood as we have been led to believe. It is lapped up in much the same way as a cat laps milk. The tongue moves in and out slowly forming a partial vacuum which aids in the flow of blood into the mouth. These bats have been known to gluttonously lap up blood for up to an hour. Having a voracious appetite means that they will consume half their body-weight in blood. Some drink so much they're hardly able to fly. Usually the poor cow is none the wiser, unless the bat infects her with rabies as a "thank you" for blood involuntarily donated.

So, why doesn't the cow jump sky-high when bitten like this? It was once thought that while biting the bat injected a type of local anaesthetic to numb the area first. This, like it or not, is not the case. For whatever reason, the slumbering bovines remain blissfully unaware of being bitten at all. Well, biting is, after all, a vampire bat's profession – they have to be good at it!

# WHAT IS A DOMESTIC ANIMAL?

Dogs and cats, as everybody knows, are domestic animals. But how did this come about? For a species to become domestic, it must be taken from its natural environment in the wild and put into a purely human environment. Here it is kept and bred for constant use in and around the house. Domestic animals satisfy basic human needs for food, clothing and companionship. They supply the raw materials for many different products and help in performing domestic chores. They are also used in medical research and occupy a very important place in human social life.

Becoming domesticated presupposes that a wild animal is suitable for the process and that people have an interest, for whatever reason, in keeping the animal. Man has attempted to domesticate many wild animals by keeping them in captivity, but captivity alone is not enough to domesticate an animal, although it may well be enough to tame it. When we go to the zoo we see animals in captivity who may be somewhat tamed, but are not in any way domesticated.

In the beginning, those animals with the smallest brain sizes, like poultry, were domesticated. The smaller the brain size, the more suitable for domestication. Being domesticated lowers an animal's adaptability to its environment. Some of its activities change: wild cats, for instance, catch and kill their prey. Domestic cats may continue to catch prey but they don't intentionally kill it and often can't be bothered with eating it. Purring, which in wild cats is only a communication between mother and kitten, is in the domestic cat a means of communicating with humans. Dogs today don't have as much to say to each other as would members of their ancestral species.

Domestication doesn't completely banish an animal's wild instincts — these are just dampened somewhat to make the animal serve its human master more efficiently.

# Why Do Animals Have Tongues?

Aquatic animals like fish have very basic tongues. Theirs are usually just a fleshy fold on the floor of their mouths, capable of very little movement. It is really only there to help push food back towards the throat for swallowing. As a fish's food is already wet, it doesn't need to be moved around the mouth for moistening before swallowing.

Some birds' tongues are a bit like this too. Again, they're very basic and just lie in the floor of their mouths. Other birds, like parrots or cockatoos, have large fleshy tongues which are used for manipulating nuts and seeds while they are being dehusked. Some very special parrots have tongues with brushes on the tip. This allows them to gather pollen and nectar from tree flowers.

A well-developed tongue is an adaptation to life on land. This is because of the many roles the tongue plays in an animal's survival. Animals such as chameleons have spectacular tongues which are used for hunting. Chameleons shoot their tongues out of their mouths at lightning speed hitting an unsuspecting insect or small bird with the tip. Because the tip is covered with a sticky substance, the prey sticks to it and is pulled straight back into the mouth. Having a tongue one-and-a-half times the length of its body helps, of course. Frogs, while performing the same trick, are less spectacular. They flip their much shorter "hinged" tongues out to catch insects and can thrust their tongues out either partially or fully, depending on how near or far the prey actually is. While a frog's tongue is useful for swallowing, it sometimes isn't enough to induce it. Some frogs have to close their eyes when they swallow, allowing their eyeballs to drop down on to the roof of their mouth and push the food into the throat.

Tongues can also be used as a means of investigation to receive information about the environment and surroundings. A snake's forked tongue can flick in and out even when its jaws are tightly shut, thanks to a tiny cleft at the front of the snake's mouth. It tastes the air and then brings in particles on its tongue for analysis. The two-pronged tongue is inserted into two little pits in the roof of its mouth, this is somewhat like having an internal nose and it plays an integral part in the recognition of food.

In many mammals, taste cells are positioned on the tongue. They make the final decision with regard to what is and what isn't to be swallowed. All mammals, except for cats which cannot distinguish sweet from other tastes, have the same general range of taste perception on their tongues. Fish, however, don't have tastebuds centred on their tongues. Their taste receptors are scattered all over the surface of their bodies.

And where would a dog be without its tongue? A dog's tongue is used for cooling down when the animal is too hot and for cleaning up after young pups. The tongue and tail are both important tools used in displays of affection. Being licked by a dog means much more than just finding out how good you taste – it also means he likes you!

# WHY ARE ANIMALS
## DIFFERENTLY COLOURED?

Hair, wool, fur, as everyone knows, the coat or **PELAGE**, comes in a variety of colours and styles. To survive, an animal must either fight its enemies or keep out of their way. Harmless, tasty, soft-bodied animals have to find some means of concealment. When attacked they either flee or hide. The rest of the time they must make themselves as inconspicuous as possible. This is why the majority of animals are not brightly coloured. They survive by avoiding trouble. The reverse, however, can also be true. Predators themselves may have dull coats to disguise their presence from prey.

Being covered with irregular patches of colour helps both in protection and in subterfuge. Mottled colours break up the outline of an animal's body so its shape is disguised. Concealing patterns help an animal resemble its environment or background. Often the same coat has to be capable of making the animal either more or less visible. This is achieved by raising and lowering the hair itself making the animal appear larger or smaller. The pelage of most terrestrial animals resembles the colour of the soil on which they live. Desert animals, for instance, are often nearly white both to reflect light, preventing the animal from overheating, and to help the creature blend in with its surroundings.

Why then are some animals brightly coloured? Well, partly for the same reasons. Warning often takes on a vivid range of colour. Dangerous animals may advertise this fact with gaudy colours. They warn enemies that they themselves are animals to be feared. Social activities often require coats emblazoned with colour. This can help attract a mate and may also be useful in frightening off the competition. In some groups, intense coloration is a status symbol helping one species distinguish itself from another with which it shares a living space.

What about animals like elephants – do they try to make themselves inconspicuous and blend in with their environment, or do they want to stand out and be seen? Elephants don't really care. These mega-herbivores don't hunt other animals, nor are they hunted – except by man. They are more interested in avoiding sunburn, hence their special colour.

# What Makes Some Eels Electric?

It has been known since the beginning of time that certain fish can deliver electric shocks. Some of these shocks are more than minor discharges. The electric eel of the Amazon basin can deliver a shock of up to 550 volts – strong enough to kill a fully-grown horse! How do they do it?

Well, there is nothing revolutionary about fish generating and discharging electricity. In all creatures, every time a muscle – large or small – contracts, there is a minute electrical discharge. Some fish have, in effect, transformed certain muscles into batteries. These battery-muscles do not contract like other muscles. Instead, their sole purpose is to generate electricity.

Electric eels have up to 6,000 of these batteries and each of them can generate about one-tenth of a volt. One may ask to what use does the electric eel put all this voltage? Very high voltages are used to stun or kill prey for food; the electric eel hunts using its batteries as ammunition.

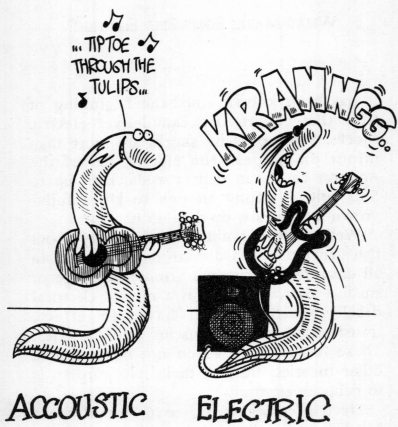

Lower voltages are also produced; their role is to help the eel navigate. An electric field is set up around its long body — a bit like the electric field that surrounds a magnet. If the eel swims near a rock or another fish, special sense organs on its skin detect distortions in the electric field due to the nearby objects. The eel has the same benefits as those fish who use sonar to find their way through murky waters at night.

The eel's electric current is also put to social uses. They communicate using electricity in much the same way as other animals use scent, sight, or acoustic signals. Internal batteries help eels recognise each other, allowing them to establish a pecking order.

Most animals interact and defend themselves using a multitude of means: sight, sound, touch, teeth and claws. The eel is fortunate in that it has discovered one system which can do the lot!

# Why Do Birds
## Have Different Beaks?

The beginning of a bird's digestive tract is the beak. Basically it's the upper and lower jaw sticking out in front of the bird's face. The beak is covered with a hard horny material to make it strong. Beaks are expertly designed for each of the many functions they perform. Because a bird's forelimbs, or wings, are of little use the beak serves as a hand. It is used in nest building, feather preening and even as a weapon. Beaks have been devised to enable their owners to avail of food and, because different species of birds have different digestive tracts, their beaks are specialised to fit the diet of the bird.

Since avians don't have teeth they can't grind or chew their food into pieces before swallowing. As a result, birds often have to swallow large mouthfuls of food and have developed specialised throats capable of processing their diet. Herring gulls, for example, can easily down a whole herring or mackerel in one gulp.

A bird's beak has to be capable not only of catching food, but also of picking it up and holding it while it is being carried away to be eaten. Thus, the shape of a bird's beak gives us a good indication of the type of food it eats. Birds of prey, like hawks or falcons, have sharp hooked beaks. Their main function is ripping food into smaller pieces which can then be swallowed. Their beaks are never used for pecking. Falcons often use their beaks to assist in killing. They have a special notch in part of the beak which, when the beak shuts, is used to break the neck of the victim.

Beak clicking is unique to owls. The upper and lower parts of the beak snap noisily against each other. This is only done when the owl is feeling angry or aggressive and is used to threaten enemies. INSECTIVOROUS birds usually have tiny beaks which are designed for picking up insects one at a time. Gannets and other fish-eaters have long pointed beaks to facilitate the catching and holding of fish. Seed-eaters' short strong beaks often have a groove on the inside. This keeps the seed in place while the shell is being removed. The famously colourful toucan beak, ideally suited to picking fruit, also acts as a communication device preventing confusion between itself and other species.

Combination beaks are also useful. They usually belong to scavengers like seagulls. Their beaks are long and pointed for catching fish, and hooked for tearing fish into bite-sized pieces.

Big beaks, wide beaks, sharp beaks – diet determines design. What would *we* be like if our mouths also changed shape depending on which foods we ate?

# How Do Spiders Use
## Their Silky Threads?

A spider's silky thread is the strongest natural fibre around and spiders can produce loads of it. Consisting of a special type of protein which doesn't dissolve in water it is produced as a sticky liquid by little glands on the spider's abdomen. The spider's many legs then pull it out into strands of various lengths. For spiders it is just a part of everyday life. Spider mothers weave silky purses for their eggs. These are called the **EGG SACS** and some spiders carry them around until the eggs inside hatch. Others aren't as devoted to their egg sacs – they just spin them and spurn them, leaving them behind. Inside, as many as 2,000 spider eggs are cushioned on the silky substance.

After the baby spiders or **SPIDERLINGS** emerge *en masse* from the egg sac they instinctively feel the need to move away to different areas. The tiny spiders climb up blades of grass or some other relatively high object and then produce long silky strands. These get caught by the breeze and carry the spiderlings considerable distances. While this ballooning or AERIAL DISPERSAL may be a spectacular method of migration, it has its dangers. The tiny spiders are at the mercy of the winds and may end up landing in unsuitable places.

The most important use of a spider's silky thread is for catching prey. Webs work because they are difficult for insects to see. Not all spiders construct webs, but those that do often make a new web each day, rolling up the old one and eating it. Various web spiders have developed a multitude of web styles and prey-catching strategies. Usually the web consists of a silky mat with a safe retreat at one end where the spider hides. Once the victim is snagged in the sticky web, the spider emerges. Before it attacks and bites its prey, out comes the sticky thread again. The spider wraps up its victim in it. Completely immobilised, the unfortunate insect is carried or hauled to a safe place for eating.

Non-web spiders sometimes use their thread as a safety-line when hunting on vertical surfaces. They abseil down walls attached to their silky safety-line. More adventurous spiders will bungee-jump off surfaces using their elastic safety-lines, enabling them to hunt in inaccessible areas.

No one could accuse spiders of sitting on their laurels and burying their talents; their enterprising skill and ingenuity with silk has made them one of the most successful species on earth.

# WHY DO HEDGEHOGS SOMETIMES
# COVER THEMSELVES WITH SPIT?

This strange behaviour, officially known as **SELF-ANOINTING**, is a rather repulsive practice in which hedgehogs often indulge. If one happens upon a lump of dog faeces or dung from another animal, it can get quite excited. After a lot of sniffing, licking and chewing, it starts drooling and salivating on the excrement. Then it begins spitting and flicking this saliva over the spines on its back and sides. The hedgehog seems to revel in this occupation and can often be found up to an hour after it began still spreading the spittle all over its body. After all this exertion the hedgehog will appear quite happy with itself and will often go off in search of food.

The question is – why do they do it? Does it make the hedgehog more attractive to the opposite sex? That would be too bizarre to be believed. Could it be done to camouflage their own smell and make them unattractive to predators? Again, there is little evidence to support this theory. Why bother daubing

themselves with faeces and spit to keep predators away when they can roll up into a bristling impenetrable spiky ball instead? Hedgehogs don't have many natural predators anyway.

It is a well-known fact that hedgehogs have fleas — could it be that this spittle has a damaging effect on the ectoparasites? Well, not really. While self-anointing may be distasteful, it is of little benefit as an insecticide.

The real reason for this strange behaviour may be quite simple — though it isn't fully known or understood. A vague guess would be that maybe they just happen to enjoy it!

# How Do Fleas Succeed
## In Their Quest For Blood?

It has happened to everyone at some stage — they have fallen victim to a flea's need for nutrition. Adult fleas, both male and female, feed on the blood of warm-blooded animals, including humans. Feeding routines depend on the species of flea. Some snack repeatedly, others consume huge volumes at irregular intervals.

Having located a victim, the flea settles on its skin and feeding starts. Frequently several attempts at finding a vein or blood-vessel are made before the flea is successful. This explains how a few fleas can cause hundreds of individual penetrations over a brief period. However, these tough little insects don't exactly bite us; instead they actually stab us with needlelike mouth parts which form a food channel or straw for the flea. When a hungry flea arrives at an appetising patch of warm skin, the action begins. It gets ready to feed by tilting its head back. A spring-like mechanism in its head releases a hammer which strikes the needle tube, forcing it through the victim's skin. This stabbing continues until the flea hits a blood-vessel and then the sucking starts. The victim of these stabbings is usually unaware of what is happening because the process is painless unless the flea hits a nerve-ending in the skin. Feeding usually lasts for a few minutes before the flea moves on to a different patch of skin or changes host altogether.

These greedy feeders only digest a small portion of what they consume. Much of the blood passes through the flea's body without being digested and is squirted from the flea's rear end. This explains what those little black flea dirts often seen on dogs and cats are. Massive numbers of fleas sucking significant amounts of blood can cause ANAEMIA. Mostly, however, blood loss is insignificant and the flea isn't begrudged its dinner.

Fleas, however, can also spread disease. This unfortunate insect was found guilty of spreading the bubonic plague centuries ago. Nowadays, it is the small amount of saliva released with each "bite" that can cause big problems. This is injected into the skin and contains ANTICOAGULANTS to help keep the blood flowing freely. The injection of this foreign fluid can cause the swollen itchy skin patches characteristic of a fleabite. These minuscule animals can live for up to six months without a drop of blood passing their mouth tube. They lurk in dark damp crevices and corners until an unsuspecting victim comes by. Then they hop out, hitch a ride and refuel themselves!

# How Do Horses See?

Horses have huge eyes, bigger than any other mammal including whales. Their eyes are perfectly positioned on either side of the head. The retina at the back of the horse's eye is a funny shape called a CAMPED RETINA. The head must be raised and lowered to help it focus on objects at various distances. This the horse does quickly — often as if it's frisking. To see something in the distance, the horse moves its head down; it swings it up again quickly to focus on an object nearby. This explains why it is so important to give a horse freedom to move its head when out riding. With its head held high, a horse can see all around itself and so can see all the others of its group and check if there are any predators in the vicinity. Its enormous eyes enable it to see fast movement and colour nearly as well as we can.

When standing straight in front of a horse you "disappear." This surprising fact is due to the horse's BLIND ZONE. This zone extends up to six feet straight in front of its face and also directly behind it. To keep you in sight, the horse will either tilt its head or walk backwards. It is well known that standing directly behind any horse is dangerous. This is because horses don't like anything moving directly behind them, especially if it is in their blind zone. Any movement in this area will be regarded as a threat, especially in an unhandled horse. If it can't turn its whole body around, or at least its head, then the chances of it kicking out are quite high.

It is vital, when jumping, that the horse can lower its head or tilt it sideways on the approach. This helps the animal to see where the actual jump is and how high it will need to spring in order to clear it. If its head movement is too restricted the horse will often charge straight into a jump as if it hasn't seen it.

Despite the fact that horses have good eyesight, they need to be allowed to see around them. When working with them apply the road safety rule: "Be safe, be seen."

# WHY ARE SKUNKS SO SMELLY?

Well, usually they're not. Skunks rely for defence on special glands in their bottoms which produce stink-bombs. They will only resort to this secret weapon in desperation and don't go around, like other animals, marking their territory by leaving their scent on trees and other objects. The skunk prefers to wander around in a leisurely manner looking for insects and other small animals to eat.

What happens if you approach a skunk? Skunks play fair. First of all, warnings will be issued. Skunks start by stamping their feet and arching their backs repeatedly, creating a vivid display of black and white fur. Sometimes, in desperation, they will stand up on their front paws in a threatening display. If you don't heed these signs as the poor animal frantically warns you to back off — then you pay!

The skunk's big tail flicks straight up in the air and, looking over its shoulder, it aims its bum in your direction. Once it has you in its

„FIRE!!!

sights — splat! — it shoots a stinking substance in your face. Its aim is usually accurate. You will immediately feel a burning sensation on your skin. If some gets into your mouth, vomiting will follow. You can be temporarily blinded if this smelly substance hits you in the eyes. Worst of all, people over a mile away will be able to smell you and the stench can linger for ages. Taking a bath in tomato juice will help diminish the smell enormously. However, you will still have to burn your clothes! Skunks don't often use this evil-smelling secretion on each other, preferring instead to fight tooth-and-claw, keeping their secret stink for enemies, not rivals.

Skunks idealistically believe that all creatures will heed their warnings. Unfortunately, they have not come to terms with the industrial age and consequently suffer high mortalities on roads. Unlike other animals, skunks will stand their ground and squirt at oncoming vehicles instead of moving out of the way. They have always been unpopular animals and some people feel that this is justified. In truth, they just want to be left alone and anyone who has been a victim of nature's stink-bomb launcher will keep this in mind the next time they spot one in the distance!

# How Do Cold-Blooded Animals Keep Warm?

Only birds and mammals are warm-blooded. This means that the body is kept warm using food as fuel. Up to 90% of the food eaten by these animals is used up just keeping warm. Cold-blooded animals like snakes or fish usually feel cold to touch. They need to be warm inside to function well. When they warm up they're active. They are, therefore, variable-blooded, heating up and cooling down frequently. Unlike warm-blooded animals they don't use food as fuel to heat the body. Instead they have other more simple methods.

Fish keep warm simply by living and swimming in water warm enough for comfort. As the water cools down or heats up so too does the temperature of the fish. This means that fish can't maintain a body temperature significantly higher or lower than the water around them.

Cold-blooded land animals, like lizards, can't generate heat from inside their bodies.

Their body temperature is controlled by their behaviour. To warm up they sunbathe; this raises their temperature well above that of the air around them. To keep themselves from overheating, they move into the shade. When feeling chilly, it's back to basking in direct sunlight. This saves energy and encourages the production of vitamin D, important for bones.

A cold-blooded animal's size and colour governs how quickly all these changes occur. Dark colours are good for absorbing heat, so cold-blooded creatures living in cooler climates usually have dark-coloured skins. When they're warm, they're active, when they're cold they get lazy. Shelter and protection is vital in the evening when they've cooled down again. This makes them less prone to being seen and caught by predators.

If you were thinking of becoming a cold-blooded animal it would be best to be a small one living in a warm climate. The bigger you were, the longer it would take you to warm up in the morning. Being a cold-blooded land animal living in the Arctic would be disastrous! This explains why most live in tropical climates.

So, what's the advantage of being cold-blooded? Well, cold-blooded creatures tend not to become overweight. Is this a bonus — what do you think?

# WHY DO DEER HAVE ANTLERS?

First things first. Antlers are not horns. They grow from a base which is part of the animal's skull. These branchy bony structures are shed each year. As the days get longer, new ones start to grow, bigger than the year before. Cartilage is the main constituent of new antlers which are covered with a skin called VELVET. This soft, felty covering contains lots of blood. Stags take great care not to damage their antlers while "in velvet" and any fighting which occurs is done by rearing up on hind legs and striking out with their front hooves. Later on in the year the velvet is rubbed off and the hard antlers, which consist only of dead bone, appear. As a stag reaches maturity, its antlers get larger with more branches or TINES.

Why have these big branchy things sticking out of the tops of their heads at all? Tough antlers are used as tools to dig for food and to mark trees. They come in very handy as weapons to fight off other rival deer who invade their territory or try to get near the

WOW!

females. But when a stag meets an enemy, any big carnivore, from whom he can't escape, he will normally defend himself by kicking out with his sharp hooves rather than use his antlers. Antlers are also important for recognition. They act like a badge and tell other deer a lot about the owner; how old he is, how strong he is and how important he is. If a stag's antlers are damaged or broken, then his fighting prowess will be diminished and he will become less important in his social hierarchy.

Reindeer are unique in deer society because female reindeer also have antlers. This helps them to compete with males for food and space in winter when snow is everywhere. It could be said that reindeer are the leaders in the quest for deer equality.

# How Do Jellyfish Sting?

Everyone knows how bees do it. A sting protrudes from the bee's body and pierces the skin injecting a tiny amount of venom. The jellyfish also has a poisonous stinger, in fact, thousands of them. While most poisonous animals are brightly coloured to warn potential victims of their danger, jellyfish are an exception. The most fatally poisonous animal in the world is a lump of jelly called a SEA WASP or BOX JELLYFISH. So, how does this soft, flabby mass actually do it?

Jellyfish are related to sea anemones; both possess a multitude of stingers which are used to capture and kill prey. They are also used as weapons of defence.

Jellyfish consist of a saucer-shaped mass with lots of thin strands or tentacles extending from its underside. The Box Jellyfish is about the size of a watermelon and its tentacles can grow up to ten feet long. Because of their fragility, the tentacles of jellyfish are easily damaged and they are very careful about protection. Situated on these tentacles are little venom bombs or capsules. Like tiny, round balls each capsule is covered in spines or barbs and full of venom. If you brush against a tentacle, the capsule lid lifts off and a barb shoots out through the opening into your skin. The venom is then discharged into your body. Symptoms from a sting like this can range from a mild prickling sensation, a bit like a nettle sting, to a shooting pain and/or loss of consciousness. If a person touches a Box Jellyfish it means certain death. The sting itself causes unbearable pain and its venom can kill a human in four minutes.

Because their diet consists of spiny animals which, if eaten alive, could tear their delicate organs, jellyfish sting their prey prior to eating it. Except for some turtles who eat them (we don't know how they manage it), most other animals know to stay away from jellyfish and you would be well advised to follow suit. When on the beach, steer well clear of all strange gelatinous animals!

# WHY DO HARES LIKE
## LIVING AROUND AERODROMES?

The common hare is a famously shy, timid and solitary creature. Yet, for some reason, hares often choose to spend time at airports! Perhaps they hope to hop on a plane and leave the country to avoid hare coursing? While this, of course, would be a valid reason for their presence at aerodromes, it is hardly likely.

One reason for them choosing to live in these noisy and dangerous places in the modern urban scene is the fact that they seem to like noise and this is as noisy a place as any! It is a well-documented fact that hares get excited and agitated during thunderstorms and spend each March making lots of noise themselves, squealing at each other and thumping their hind feet on the ground. Having said this, their noise-making and the roaring sound of jets taking off and landing is not a realistic comparison. The engines make noise which would be uncomfortably loud for the poor hares, yet they continue to hang out in these places.

"WOW! WOULD YOU LOOK AT THE EARS ON THAT GUY!!!"

Could it be that the grass growing between the runways is extra tasty and irresistible? It would definitely be worth suffering all the noise for the succulent grass this land provides. However, even if the grass were excellent, it would still not explain why such solitary creatures overcome their shyness to spend time *en masse* at these places . . .

The hares, in fact, probably like the sight of the planes themselves. Demonstrating their speed is one of the hare's strongest instincts of self-expression. One theory has it that hares have an inbuilt instinct to challenge other fast-moving objects even though other animals would be completely freaked out by the noise. Who could argue that the sleek planes flying in and out of airports meet this challenge!

# WHICH ANIMALS SLEEP THE MOST?

Every living animal needs to sleep for regular intervals in each period of 24 hours. We sleep about one-third of our lives away, or for around eight hours a day. Other animals' sleeping patterns vary from ours. Sloths, for example, sleep for at least 20 hours per day, whereas the giraffe can survive quite happily on just two hours. Goats never seem to sleep. They just lie on the ground with their eyes open. When they become drowsy their ears droop slightly, but any slight sound will instantly alert them. The common swift never rests in the usual way. It sleeps "on the wing", taking very short naps while gliding and flying.

Another animal insomniac is the sooty tern, a sea bird that lives mostly far from land. Its feet are not webbed so it cannot land on the water to feed or rest. It just swoops down and picks up fish swimming near the surface of the water. It rests by sleeping on the wing like a swift. Because birds in general have so many predators, most can't afford the luxury of extended periods of deep sleep.

Other animals, also at the mercy of predators, sleep in hide-outs. Bats sleep deeply in the eaves of roofs, hollow tree trunks or in caves. Some spend about half the year in hibernation. For the other half, they sleep all day coming out to feed at dusk. Then it's back to sleep till dawn when they come out to feed for an hour or so again. Some may sleep day and night for about six months of the year, twenty-two hours a day during the remaining six months.

This sleepy record is matched only by a resident of New Zealand, a lizard called the Tuatara. It also sleeps for six months of the year and stays in its burrow the rest of the year. It is so dozy that it often falls asleep while chewing its food. Tuataras, as you might imagine, move very slowly, but can live for over 100 years! However, by sleeping most of their lives away they do miss out on a lot . . . well, as much as a lizard can miss out on!

# WHAT WOULD HAPPEN IF ANIMALS COULDN'T SMELL?

Smell is the perception of airborne chemicals that are inhaled when creatures breathe. It was probably the first of the senses to develop, and we now know that the lives of many animals — from insects to mammals — are governed by this sense. It is used in feeding, detecting enemies, recognising mates and offspring, and in courtship and in rivalry. But if animals couldn't smell, then:

- Tomcats wouldn't spray urine
- Dogs wouldn't cock their legs at lampposts
- Snakes wouldn't have forked tongues that flick in and out
- Salmon wouldn't be able to find their way home
- Foxes would always escape from foxhounds
- Male bees or drones wouldn't be attracted to the Queen Bee
- Male moths wouldn't be able to attract female moths from miles away
- Ants and termites wouldn't be able to find food

I'M NOT INTERESTED!

- Stallions wouldn't find mares attractive
- Otters wouldn't be able to prove ownership of their homes or territories
- Hamsters would have less confidence when put into new cages
- Hippos wouldn't wave their tails from side to side when defecating
- Baby barnacles wouldn't be able to find their parents and family on rocks
- Rabbits' social lives would be severely disrupted
- Skunks would have to develop another method of defence

And so on . . .

# How Is It That Fish
## Appear Weightless In Water?

A human diver with simple breathing apparatus can enjoy the freedom that fish have had for millions of years — weightlessness in water. Thanks to SCUBA gear, man is now able to hover at any depth with no effort, balancing his tendency to float or sink using weights and a buoyancy vest. Fish, on the other hand, are born with inbuilt devices called **SWIM BLADDERS**.

The swim bladder develops as an outgrowth of the intestines and becomes a gas-filled balloon below the backbone. It makes up around seven per cent of a fresh water fish's total volume, five per cent in seawater fish. The swim bladder inflates or deflates depending on whether the fish wants to swim down towards the seabed or up towards the surface. It also helps fish to stay poised in midwater with little or no effort and completely eliminates weight in water.

Not all fish have one of these special organs. Flatfish, like plaice or sole, don't have swim bladders. Because they live on the sea or river bed, buoyancy is not a big issue. Bigger fish like sharks also lack this gas pouch. They're heavier than seawater and would soon sink if they relaxed their efforts. Instead, they have huge livers filled with a special fat called SQUALENE. Fat floats, but they need lots of it to help them stay buoyant and have to keep swimming all the time. Their skeletons are not made up of bones, as you would expect, but of cartilage which is lighter than bone.

So, swim bladders are not the only device for helping fish stay weightless in water. Nevertheless, having one relieves a fish of continued energy loss and seems a far better alternative to having a fatty liver!

# WHY DO WHALES HAVE NOSTRILS
## ON TOP OF THEIR HEADS?

Fish don't need to come to the surface of the water to breathe air the way that whales do. When swimming and diving, whales must hold their breath, resurfacing at intervals to expel the used air and to take in a new breath. They can dive down a kilometre towards the deep seabed and stay underwater for up to two hours on one breath!

Whales are mammals and most mammals have their nostrils on their faces. Because these giants live in water, coming up to the surface only to breathe, breathing in and out has been facilitated by nature's moving the nostrils from the front of the face to the top of the head. Thus the whale's nostrils are also its **BLOWHOLE**!

To stop water from getting into the blowhole while the whale is submerged, a nasal plug acts like a cork-stopper, blocking water out. As the whale returns to the surface, its lungs gradually expand and the nasal plug is forced open so that all the old breath can be released. It bursts out noisily and appears as a cloud of spray. The whale then immediately inhales with great gusto and glides beneath the water head first. Whales fill their lungs to capacity every time and can hold their breath up to twenty times as long as any terrestrial animal.

Whales cannot breathe through their mouths. Due to a specially developed larynx, food and air passages are totally separate and distinct. The blowholes have a continuous passage to the lungs which enables them to feed underwater. If the whale had the same arrangement of windpipes and tubes as ourselves, it would drown trying to feed as water would get into its lungs. Having nostrils on top of its head is obviously the best arrangement for the whale and just another of nature's little miracles!

# Why Do Birds Sing?

The sounds birds make are usually, though not always — as anyone who has heard a crow will agree — musical. Their songs come from the SYRINX which is a small voicebox at the lower end of a bird's windpipe. It has muscles both outside and inside. A bird's voicebox is very different to our own. Yet, many birds can learn to mimic human speech due to their highly developed sense of imitation.

The main reason for birdsong is advertising: A male bird will fly around the boundaries of his own territory, perching and singing every so often, letting other birds know that this is his domain and that he is ready to defend it. Male birds of the same species are told to keep out while females are invited in by the very same song. The male usually stops singing after the female has laid her eggs.

Some birds prefer to perch in foliage in the woods where, hidden from predators, they can sing long continuous songs without

interruption. These birds can advertise while simultaneously being inconspicuous to predators. Their songs are usually the loudest and, to us, sound the best. These singers generally have dull feathers and blend in with the woodland colours. Some woodland birds have quiet songs not meant for the whole neighbourhood to hear. They're sung to ensure that male and female birds stay together. Other birds prefer to sing in exposed sites. Their songs are shorter and choppier because they must keep a look-out and listen for danger while singing. Birds usually have their own favourite singing sites called **SONG POSTS** which tend to be situated right in the middle of their territory. They sing best when relaxed, not when they are being hunted or hassled by anything.

As everyone knows, lots of different species of bird can live in any one area – all singing and advertising their presence. Consequently, they must each have different songs to avoid confusion. This has led to the development of more and more complex songs which are loudest at dawn and dusk. To humans these sound like a chorus of numerous birds all chirping together – the dawn chorus. Luckily, birds can understand all these chirpings, separating out the individual sounds, deciphering what they mean.

Frequently, when birds are in sight of each other, they don't communicate with song. Instead, information is conveyed through movement and plumage — a bit like us really, but we use speech, body language and clothing!

# What Happens When
# Cows Chew The Cud?

Cattle are natural **VEGETARIANS**. Their digestive systems are designed for handling huge amounts of coarse grass. Using the tongue, lips and lower front teeth (they have no upper front teeth), food is taken into the mouth. Minor chewing occurs before swallowing and the animal is on to its next mouthful! The previous bite is sent to the first of the cow's multi-chambered stomachs: the **RETICULUM**. When the reticulum fills up with grass, the cow usually sits down and appears to be resting. This is where the action begins! For the next forty-five minutes or so, "chewing the cud" or **RUMINATION** is what she concentrates on.

Cows are often observed sitting amongst their herdmates with a distant look in their eyes, chewing and chewing and chewing. What's going on? If you look closely at the animal's neck you will see a lump rise up to her throat every so often. The arrival of this lump seems to jump-start the chewing process again. After about thirty chews, the lump will slide down her neck as she swallows and before long another lump rises and the process continues.

What's happening is that the grass that she gulped down earlier in the day and stored in her reticulum is being chewed up properly for the first time. Small amounts are REGURGITATED or sent back up to the mouth. The juices in the lump of grass are squeezed out and swallowed. Each lump is then chewed up properly before being swallowed again for the second and final time.

This food doesn't return to the reticulum but makes its way to the RUMEN, or second stomach, instead. The rumen is like a big fermentation vat. It is full of fluid, bacteria and microbes. This is where the grass starts to release all its nourishment. Gas is also released in the rumen — lots of it. Every two minutes or so the cow belches to release stomach gas. You won't hear these belches because she releases them silently. Nature has perfected this whole process.

In the wild very little ever goes wrong. On farms, however, lots can go wrong with "chewing-the-cud." Specially concentrated foods are given to cows and bullocks to make them produce more milk or gain weight faster. This is where trouble can start and the vet is often sent for to help the animals with indigestion.

It's not just bovines that have multichambered stomachs: cows do it, sheep do it, even llamas on their knees do it, they all do it, they all chew the cud!

# How Can A Snake Swallow A Pig Whole?

Snakes are **CARNIVORES**. They always eat what they kill — whole. Having no limbs means that they cannot tear their food into smaller pieces, much as we do with a knife and fork. So, a snake eating a meal is like you or me swallowing a melon whole! To enable a snake to eat in this fashion the skin and skull have special adaptations.

The fangs of venomous snakes are designed for piercing the victim's body. The teeth of non-venomous snakes are pointed and designed for grabbing and holding on to prey while it is being swallowed whole. Their teeth are of no use for chewing because they have no roots. As the swallowing procedure commences, the snake's scaly face literally comes to pieces. The lower jaw splits in the middle and slides off from the rest of the skull, turning the mouth, effectively, into a large sac. The joints of the upper jawbones are very loose. They work together with a complex system of muscles and ligaments that enable the ingestion of large animals.

When eating an animal, such as a pig, for instance, the snake's rhythmic jaw movements force the animal into the throat where powerful muscles force it down into the snake's body. Breathing continues without interruption while this huge meal is being stuffed down thanks to the snake's windpipe which moves up and sticks out the side of its mouth, somewhat like a snorkel. Some snakes have no difficulty in passing struggling meals down their throats. Others prefer to subdue their meal first by poisoning or suffocating it. Eating an animal whole means that a snake's digestive juices must be very powerful, strong enough to digest bones, teeth and eggshells.

The disadvantages of such enormous mouthfuls are obvious. The snake is vulnerable to attack from enemies while its mouth is jammed with a large animal. Having eaten, however, the snake won't need to think about food for weeks!

## How Do Hedgehogs Roll Themselves Up Into Balls?

Along with their spines and fleas, hedgehogs are famous for their ability to turn their bodies into prickly balls – it's easy to do once you know how. However, don't try this at home without parental supervision!

Only the backs, foreheads and sides of hedgehogs are spiny. They have soft fur on their undercarriage and also on their legs. This is just as well because if they were completely prickly it wouldn't be possible to roll up as they do, but then again in that case it probably wouldn't be necessary.

Where the fur of the belly meets the spines of the back is a very specialised area in the hedgehog. Here they have a long stringy muscle under their skin. This contracts and tightens, pulling the loose skin of the back down over its belly. This spiny skin is also pulled over its head like a hood and its bottom tucks itself in also becoming covered. Thus, in effect, the hedgehog places itself in a sack of its own skin with spines on the outside. As all these muscles are contracting to stretch the skin, little muscles which are attached to each spine are also pulled so that the spines bristle and criss-cross forming an impenetrable barrier. The hedgehog can stay curled up in a ball like this for hours.

This is what they are supposed to do when danger threatens. In reality, hedgehogs are lazy creatures and often can't be bothered with all the effort. Generally, they just jerk their heads out of sight between their front legs. This jerking causes the spines on the back to bristle. But because of their dislike for physical exertion, hedgehogs will often just scurry under a bush instead!

# Why Do Giant
# Pandas Seem So Lazy?

The giant panda, like all bears, is a **CARNIVORE**. It has strong jaw muscles and sharp teeth like any other flesh-eating mammal. Yet it tends not to eat other animals and usually prefers plants. Why has this carnivore turned vegetarian? Bamboo is a clue to the giant panda's behaviour. Pandas live in China where there is an abundance of this specialised grassy plant. An evergreen, it is unpalatable to most other animals. As a result, the panda has food in winter when every other food source is in short supply and there is no need for pandas to hibernate as most other bears do.

The giant panda has strong teeth and powerful jaw muscles. These are necessary to crush and chew bamboo. However, its short carnivore gut cannot digest bamboo as well as a long herbivore gut can. To compensate for this shortcoming, the panda needs to eat huge quantities. It can spend up to eight hours a day feeding, often lying down to eat, followed by a nap. As if this wasn't awkward enough, it must also spend most of the night feasting on bamboo shoots just to survive!

Even after spending most of each twenty-four hour period eating, it still only has barely enough energy to live. Because bamboo in general is not very nutritious or digestible, the panda sniffs out and selects young shoots which it can digest more efficiently. Lying down to eat may appear to be the height of laziness, but for the poor panda it's a necessary energy saving ritual. This method uses less energy than sitting or standing. These big animals haven't forgotten their carnivore ancestry — it's just that they are far too slow to catch prey for themselves. If they happen to come across a carcase, they will tuck in willingly and devour it completely. This unexpected meal gives them a vitamin and energy boost. Unfortunately, the panda doesn't enjoy such luxury very often.

Only rarely does the giant panda get to eat what it was intended to and it is therefore never very energetic. To make matters worse, giant pandas are perpetually thirsty. Because of their vegetarian diet the bears lose more water in their faeces than is derived from feeding and must even drink four to five times a night. It really is a wonder that giant pandas get through the day at all!

# WHY DO ELEPHANTS PURR?

Until quite recently it was thought that elephants could control their stomach rumblings. This was because elephant hunters used to tell of whole herds having rumbly tummies, noisy one minute, quiet the next.

Then the truth was discovered. These rumblings were not from the stomach at all. They come from the elephant's voicebox, from the same part of the throat responsible for producing a cat's purr. The question is, why would an elephant purr one minute and then suddenly stop?

If an elephant becomes separated from the rest of his group while feeding in a densely wooded area, it starts making this sound in its throat. The noise then reverberates throughout its large body which actually amplifies it. The rest of the elephants hear this purring sound and purr back. It is a way of keeping in touch with one another. As long as each elephant can hear this sound, it knows that it is neither lost nor alone.

This loud purring is also used as an alarm

GERROFF!.. IT WAS BAD ENOUGH WHEN YOU JUST PURRED....

signal. An elephant which has been feeding and purring to keep in contact with the rest of its group, will suddenly stop if it senses danger. This cessation is seen as an alarm bell by the other elephants and a warning will spread through the whole herd.

Alarms like this are only necessary if the herd are in the middle of thick foliage in a wooded area. If they are feeding on open grassland where they can see each other, purring does not occur. This sudden cessation of purring among elephants at the first sign of danger is quite bizarre. Most animals make noise when alarmed; elephants do the opposite. Silence is their warning of danger.

At the first sign of danger, members of family units bunch together with the young elephants protected at the centre. Once the young elephants sense that danger has passed they begin meowing to each other — only joking!

# WHAT IS COUNTER-SHADING?

The most common colour pattern in all fish is
**COUNTER-SHADING**. Usually, light shining from
above makes the fish's back more brightly lit
than its belly. If the fish were all the one
colour and shade, its underside would seem
very dark compared to its well-illuminated
back and sides. Counter-shading compensates
for this. The back is usually a deeper hue
than the sides which fade to a pale underside
so that shadows aren't apparent — just look at
a salmon or mackerel!

What is the reason for this? All animals,
including fish, have three-dimensional bodies.
It's their solid shape that makes them easily
seen. If they appear flat and two-dimensional
they seem less visible and less animal-like.
This increases their chances of successfully
escaping from predators and also their chances
of catching other animals. Fish that show
marked counter-shading live in bright surface
waters and feed on other smaller fish and
squid. Silvery fish have the best camouflage,
even better than that of counter-shaded fish.

Many fish and aquatic animals have stripes which disrupt their colour pattern by cutting across the body, disguising fins and flippers. This confuses their general shape. Dark circles around the eyes aren't a sign of tiredness in marine life. Their presence conceals the eyes and protects against glare.

Not every aquatic animal needs counter-shading. The great white whale is too large to worry about hiding from predators. It feeds on plankton, tiny aquatic plants too short-sighted to see the whale anyway! Generally speaking, whales don't need to hide from predators, yet their colour pattern is often counter-shaded and mottled. This is to make capturing prey easier for the whale, not to protect them from enemies. Their coloured lines direct attention away from their mouth thus deceiving their prey, giving them the advantage.

For us counter-shading is nature's way of making animals more interesting to look at and means that below the surface, nothing is as it appears to be.

# ARE CUCKOO MOTHERS UNCARING?

Some people think that cuckoos are bad mothers because they seldom rear their own chicks. Lots of female cuckoos rely on other birds to care for their young. But perhaps the cuckoo is not as irresponsible as we might think. She has developed very clever methods of ensuring the care of her eggs and baby chicks. After watching for other small birds to finish building their nests, she waits for them to start laying. Then, when the nest is left unattended she makes her move . . .

Egg laying can be a long process and birds must often sit and wait for some time before an egg finally appears. The cuckoo does not have time for this. Her eggs must be laid quickly before the owner of the nest returns. The female cuckoo swoops down over each nest and quickly deposits an egg into each one. Cuckoo eggs have very tough shells which prevent them smashing or cracking when they land. Outwardly her eggs look similar to the eggs already in the nest. This throws the other birds off the trail and, though some may cop on and remove the cuckoo's egg or desert the nest, most don't seem to notice anything unusual. However, they often attack the female cuckoo if they catch her in the act. Cuckoo females continue depositing eggs into various nests until the whole clutch is laid. They have been known to remove an existing egg from the nest before theirs is laid so that the numbers remain constant. That's it! Maternal duties are finito!

The unsuspecting stepmother bird incubates both her own as well as the impostor's egg. If all goes according to plan, the cuckoo's egg hatches first. The chick may proceed to dispose of all the other eggs in the nest. That way it gets all the food and attention for itself. Other cuckoo chicks don't bother kicking the others out, they just grow faster than the other nestlings and starve them out. Such bullying tactics ensure that the cuckoo grows into a strong fledgling quickly. After three weeks or so, the cuckoo leaves the nest, but its foster-parents continue to feed it. They − being small birds in comparison − often have to perch on the young cuckoo's back in order to reach its mouth!

So, maybe the cuckoo mother isn't uncaring at all. She arranges for each of her young to have the individual and undivided attention of a stepmother. Her young get more food and better care than she could ever provide . . .

# Why Is A Frog's
## Skin So Moist?

Frogs have very thin skin. Moisture is produced by lots of tiny glands in the skin. These work continuously and in hot weather go into overdrive covering the frog with a layer of slime. This helps prevent sunburn and keeps the frog in a healthy uncooked state. Having damp skin, frogs also have a preference for wet, soggy places. Frogs can't drink the way you and I do. Instead, frogs satisfy all their water needs by sitting in or near it. Unlike our skin, a frog's isn't waterproof. Water can pass in and out quite easily. The rate at which it passes through varies, depending on the humidity of the environment. Because of this frogs don't do well in dry desert-like conditions. Toads, on the other hand, don't have a problem with this. They drink in the usual way and have dry skin which, like ours, is quite waterproof.

All frogs need oxygen. They can get it from the air using their lungs or take full advantage of their dewy skin and use it for breathing. Just like water, air can also pass through their skin. Skin-breathing is comparable to lung-breathing. Oxygen is taken in and carbon dioxide is sent out. The lining of the frog's mouth can also be used. Frogs can breathe by letting air into their mouths where oxygen is absorbed through the roof of the mouth. Ordinary day-to-day requirements for air are met by both the skin and the mouth. Lungs come into play only when the need for oxygen is great. Skin-breathing is particularly beneficial when frogs are sleeping on the bottom of the pond. They can stay there indefinitely, there is no need to surface. A frog's moist skin facilitates drinking and breathing, but having moist skin is also important for something else . . . it keeps them looking young!

# Why Is Dog
## Man's Best Friend?

Man's association with the dog began nearly ten thousand years ago. How did the relationship begin? We can't be too sure. The dog is probably descended from the wolf. One theory maintains that it is the wolf's personality which holds the key to understanding the strong bond between man and dog.

The wolf and early man had a lot in common. Both hunted in packs. Both communities were very organised, consisting of families with tight bonds, each member having a specific role. Perhaps primitive man saw how effectively wolves hunted and copied their technique. Young cubs were often reared by human families so that the young wolf saw the human family as its own as it grew to maturity, becoming loyal and devoted to them.

Despite the huge differences in size, shape and colour of dogs, they are all of the same species. Because dogs have interacted with

man for thousands of years, he has had plenty of time to mix them into different breeds, moulding the species to suit his needs. We have hunting dogs, guard dogs, sporting dogs, sheepdogs, toy dogs and lapdogs. When they were being bred, the calmer, tamer dogs were chosen so that a lot of the aggression that was evident in their ancestors was bred out of them. Nowadays, working dogs aren't as popular as pet dogs which are kept because they give us a feeling of companionship and closeness to nature. They provide us with an opportunity to play and give us unconditional love. We now think that dog-owners live longer than those without. Dogs have a very calming effect which reduces stress and consequently the risk of heart attacks. They are the only animal capable of showing happiness in small ways — tail-wagging is their version of laughter. Dogs are great companions for young children and elderly people and we can often see in dogs characteristics which we would like to see in other people.

Dogs may have started out as man's "best friend", but through the ages the loyalty of this rather special species has made it the "best friend of the whole human race!"

# WHY ARE FISH
## COVERED WITH SLIME?

When you touch a fish in a fish shop or hold it in your hand, it feels clammy and slimy. This is because, alive or recently dead, fish are covered with a slimy coating. This slimy layer is very important to a fish's wellbeing. Fish handlers are very careful about how they touch the fish so as not to damage or rub off any of the slippery outer surface. This slimy covering is continuously produced by fish throughout their lives by tiny glands in their skin called **MUCOUS GLANDS**. It covers their whole body and helps stop dead fish from going bad quickly in a fish shop.

Fish slime or **MUCOUS** is very like the white of an egg. Without it life would be different for the fish. Why is it so important? Well, firstly this shiny coat is crucial as a protective device for keeping bacteria and parasites at bay. Also, without this sleek top layer, swimming would be much more of an effort. The more slime the better the swimmer! Fish can move at greater speed while using up less energy. Whales, which are mammals, not fish, aren't covered with slime. Instead they have a chemical lubricant on their skin which helps them move through the sea. In filthy murky water the slimy cloak greatly enhances a fish's chances of survival by preventing dirt from adhering to its body and gills. Slime also acts like a wound-dressing if the fish has cut or damaged its skin. It helps the new skin to grow underneath.

This outer shiny film makes life so much easier for fish that, if it is removed or damaged, some fish may actually die!

# HAVE BATS MET THEIR
# MATCH IN MOTHS?

Every evening insect-eating bats leave their roosts and go hunting. Because it is dark and their eyesight is poor they must find their food using special radar or ULTRASOUND. These bats have a special voicebox which produces high-pitched squeaks. These sounds don't come out of the bat's mouth, but through its often strangely-shaped nostrils. Their squeaks echo off objects ranging from trees to insects; this is how these bats find their way around and hunt. We can't hear these ultrasonic sounds – neither can most animals – which gives the bat a huge advantage over most of its prey, except for moths!

Most moths have ears, not on the sides of their head as you might expect, but on their bodies. These ears don't hear everything, but one sound they are tuned into are the bat's ultrasonic noises. Moths can actually locate the bat before it locates them. This gives them the advantage and helps them keep out of the bat's flight path. If the bat is still quite far away the moth will zigzag off in the opposite direction or it may just dive randomly. These unexpected movements make it difficult for the bat to follow.

Moths have developed other precautions to ensure that they don't wind up inside a bat's belly. To confuse the hunting bat, a moth will emit its own high frequency sounds. These match those of the bat, totally puzzling it. The bat's echo location system "crashes" and the moth escapes.

Others emit ultrasonic clicks which we now know scare bats. These sounds probably tell the approaching bat to "back off or you'll get food poisoning." This is a good example of brains beating brawn.

One would think that moths, like most insects, would stand no chance against the bat's efficient hunting apparatus. Well, these moths just "ain't gonna take it lying down . . . "

# What Do Earthworms Actually Eat?

Most wild animals spend a considerable amount of time searching for food — but not earthworms! These **OMNIVORES**, which will eat pretty much anything, get their food from the earth itself: plants, roots, leaves, seeds and microscopic animals. Dung can even provide them with a meal. They grip their food by holding it against the roof of their mouths with a special pincer-like attachment. This enables them to pull it from the surface of the earth into little burrows where it is stored and eaten later. Night-time usually finds them slithering out of their burrows searching for leaves which they pull back with them below the surface. They may also eat the leaves of living plants. However, before embarking on this type of meal they usually squirt special fluids on to the leaves to help soften them, making them easier to eat.

Once food is in the worm's mouth, the **PHARYNX**, a kind of suction-pump, sucks food into the throat ready for swallowing. When

swallowed it heads straight for the CROP, a little storage sac inside the worm. It stays there until it passes into the GIZZARD where it is mashed up with bits of gravel before it is fully digested. This gravel has previously been eaten and believe it or not, this greatly aids an earthworm's digestion!

A worm cast is then excreted which can often be seen as a little squiggle of soil on the ground – a bit like the sandy casts lugworms leave on the beach when the tide is out. These casts help break up and enrich the soil even though their presence on well-kept lawns isn't welcomed by everyone. Earthworms spend lots of time wriggling around in the soil. While burrowing, their mouths are wide open and as they move forward, soil and mulch is forced into their mouths and passes through them and out the other end. This loosens the soil. However, earthworms are much fussier than we would imagine and don't eat bits of debris indiscriminately. If they find themselves in soil which is unsuitably hard or contains food they don't relish, they simply turn around and look elsewhere.

# What Really Happens
## At Hibernation?

One way of getting through the long winter months is to go to sleep. It must work well, judging by the number of species that choose this option. Coming from the Latin word for winter quarters, **HIBERNATION** is what this winter sleep is called. This extended slumber has many variations. True hibernation is restricted to warm-blooded animals. This restriction, however, doesn't stop cold-blooded animals from having a long sleepy rest for a few months as well.

Important preparations begin inside the animal's body a few weeks before cold weather sets in. Usually the animal gains weight in the form of fat — **BROWN FAT** as opposed to the more common **WHITE FAT**. This special fat will enable the animal to survive the winter without food.

The time then comes to find a suitable place for a long undisturbed rest. Bears go to caves. Snakes go underground. Hedgehogs bury themselves in leaves. Bats choose damp caves, while tortoises dig holes or go to cosy boxes in the utility room. When they have settled into a good sleeping position, internal changes occur. Their body processes slow down — ageing basically stops. Their heartbeat slows down and body temperature drops. Hibernating animals don't stop regulating their body temperature — they just turn down the thermostat. Bears, however, don't let their body temperature drop very low because they would never wake up again. To be accurate, bears don't hibernate. Instead, they indulge in "winter dormancy." If they hibernated properly they would die of the cold.

Hibernation is not just one long sleep. If it gets too cold outside, the animal may wake up. Bats, for instance, frequently wake up and go for a drink of water and a pee. Provided all goes well, an internal alarm clock starts ringing the following spring and all these late sleepers wake up and emerge from their sleeping-quarters looking a bit tired, thin and scrawny. They have spring and summer to look forward to and enjoy.

Winter sleep has a lot going for it. Hibernating animals usually live much longer than those who suffer the winter. There's a lesson for us there somewhere!

## WHY DO RODENTS
## GRIT THEIR TEETH?

How is it that one never sees a rat or guinea pig with dentures? This may be, in part, because they have teeth which never fall out. Their front teeth or incisors are very important for food gathering and it is vital that their teeth last as long as they do.

A rodent's front teeth are unique in that they have open roots. What this means is that, unlike our own teeth which stop growing at a certain stage in our lives, rodents teeth will continue to grow continuously throughout their lives — often at an alarming rate. If left to grow unchecked, a guinea pig's teeth may grow up to ten inches in one year! This could cause major problems for the guinea pig, so to keep them at just the right length, it grits its teeth together. This constant gritting also ensures that the teeth keep the sharp edges necessary for eating. Gnawing can blunt incisors; gritting sharpens them up again.

However, there can be difficulties. For teeth-gritting to work properly, the upper and lower front teeth must meet perfectly when the rodent shuts its jaws. This, unfortunately, isn't always the case. If the animal's upper jaw is overshot or undershot, problems arise because the teeth don't meet when chewing or gritting and, as a result, they don't wear down. Instead, they continue to grow until the upper incisors pierce the lower jaw and *vice versa*. The poor animal cannot eat and starves to death.

When this nasty problem occurs in pet rodents, the owner usually notices that there is something wrong with their pet. It may not be eating properly and is obviously in some discomfort. They bring their animal to the veterinarian who will file the front teeth down until they are at their normal level where eating can once again become a pleasure and not a problem. The filing doesn't hurt — the animal doesn't seem to mind at all. However, this procedure may have to be performed quite frequently as it tends to be a recurring problem in rodents.

So, gritting is a daily activity for most rodents. It may also ease boredom and could even be a form of communication. It also ensures proper dental care of their valuble teeth. If only our own dental care was as easy!

## Why Do Some Penguins Waddle Around With Eggs On Their Feet?

If there were prizes for making life difficult, there is no doubt that the award would surely go to the emperor penguin!

This quirky penguin lives in the Antarctic – not the warmest place in the world – and while other smaller penguins breed in spring, the emperor penguin's breeding season commences at the start of winter.

A male and female establish that they are right for one another, usually after the female accepts an engagement pebble offered by the male. A territory is then marked out, often on an ice shelf in the middle of the ocean. On this desolate site, the female penguin lays an egg before promptly waddling off into the sea to feed. This is no mere snack – she dines in style, feeding constantly for around two months, leaving the male holding the baby, or in this case, the egg . . .

As no nest is built, the male penguin has to take the egg with him wherever he waddles. This he does by simply placing it on

his feet and carrying on with the business of living. To stop it from rolling off, the egg is cleverly tucked under a little flap of skin which hangs down from the male penguin's belly — the females also have one. Lots of expectant penguin fathers are in the same predicament. They keep each other company and huddle together in blizzards to stay as warm as possible.

Some weeks later, the female penguin returns from feasting and the egg is eagerly passed over to her allowing her starving mate to head off on a feeding binge of his own.

This egg-toting does not end when the egg hatches out. The new-born baby penguin must be kept very warm to avoid freezing to death. It snuggles on Mother's or Father's feet until big enough to leave home and terminate the lease, so to speak!

# How Do Horses
## Sleep Standing Up?

Horses are jumpy. Their response to a lot of things is to kick out or to run off. This they do famously well because of the powerful muscles placed high up their legs. Preparing for movement involves all the muscles contracting and lifting the body off the ground. Powerful legs enable the horse to move quickly at the slightest sign of danger. In order to avoid being caught out, horses have developed a way of sleeping while standing. This doesn't mean that they never lie down; of course they do, but only when they feel very safe and secure. Horses are social animals and can relax far easier in groups where one horse can keep watch all the time. When put into a strange field on his own, a horse will remain standing for several days.

So, why don't they get exhausted and fall over? The answer is in their unique legs. Horses possess a bracing support system called a **STAY APPARATUS**. Found only in horses, this device consists of tendons, ligaments and muscles which prevent the legs from buckling when the horse is asleep. The joints lock into position and the legs become rigid. Very little muscular activity is needed to support the animal's weight.

If we were able to lock our legs and snooze in a standing position, our legs would soon tire from holding us up. Thanks to the stay apparatus, this doesn't happen to horses. However, if a horse is forced to stand continuously for ages, it will deprive itself of sleep and will eventually need to lie down and sleep to recover. Foals, like all young animals, need lots of sleep. They can afford to lie down and sleep securely because they know mother is standing over and protecting them. Fortunately, because the mare isn't always going to be around to protect them as they get older, the stay apparatus helps them to keep going.

# How Do Starfish Move?

Just because they are shaped like the spokes of a wheel doesn't mean that starfish move by cartwheeling along the seabed. Starfish have a much more subtle manner of moving. Having five or ten arms, they do extremely well in the arm department but lack a head and brain completely. All the action is confined to the arms themselves and to the centre where they all meet – the mouth. On the underside of each arm is a central channel running its entire length. This central groove is bordered by rows and rows of tiny finger-like tube feet. These tiny tubes move constantly, wafting back and forth in search of something solid to touch. Starfish move forward by using these little tubes.

How is it done? Each of these mini-feet fills with seawater. They then expand and stretch, moving constantly until they touch something new and solid. Then they flatten and act like thousands of tiny individual suckers. This pulls the starfish forwards, backwards, or sideways. If a tortoise is turned on to its back, it finds it nearly impossible to right itself. Thanks to the rows and rows of tiny suckers, being turned upside-down doesn't pose a problem for the starfish. It simply turns the tip of one of its arms over so that the little suckers can poke out and touch something solid. The entire arm is slowly turned over in this way. The other arms follow suit enabling the starfish to somersault into proper position.

These agile little feet attached to a starfish's arms are unique in the animal kingdom. No other animal has the tubed feet starfish have. With rows and rows of them you'd think the starfish would be a fast mover. Only moving at a rate of about 30 feet per hour, starfish could hardly be called speed freaks of the seabed!

# What Do Vultures Eat?

Being carnivorous, vultures are meat-eating birds of prey. They are unique in that they feed on dead animals. This means that they don't have to kill their prey, although newborn or defenceless animals wouldn't be totally safe with hungry vultures around. Unlike other birds of prey, vultures are not adapted to fighting. A vulture's feet and claws are comparatively weak. Their tricks of the trade are, however, quite ingenious.

Having a huge wingspan enables them to spend lots of time in the air, scanning for snacks. Because they are rather large, ungainly birds, able to flap their wings only for very short periods, they depend on rising warm air currents to lift them to high altitudes when flying. Often they will be up so high they can't distinguish whether or not an animal on the ground is dead. Keeping an eye peeled for other scavengers such as jackals, crows, hyenas, helps them decide when or when not to dive down. If their interest is aroused they will begin to circle lower and lower. This sends a signal to other airborne scavengers to home in also. Vultures can swoop down at speeds of up to one hundred miles an hour and land beside the dead animal where feeding can commence.

Having a poor sense of smell means that vultures are not sickened by the often rotting food they eat. For hygienic purposes, the head and neck of the vulture are usually bald; it would otherwise get soiled with blood as the vulture pokes its head deeply into a carcase. Because of a tendency to live in hot climates, constant exposure to sun prevents bacterial growth on their head and necks. Clean by nature, vultures bathe and preen after feeding. Even the act of defecating down their legs is for a good hygienic purpose. Vulture faeces have disinfectant properties which keeps their legs clean.

How is it that after eating rotten food they don't get food poisoning? Vultures have very strong digestive juices in their stomachs which kill all bacteria and other toxins. These juices are strong enough to digest bones. As well as feeding on dead cattle, llamas and sheep, vultures sometimes eat stranded marine mammals like whales, or people too, if they can find them. These birds have also been known to drive animals off clifftops to their death and then devour them. They can frequently be seen flying into the air with

"SICK OF CARRION, BOB DECIDED IT WAS TIME TO GET SOMETHING FRESH!"

bones held in their beaks or claws. These they drop on to rocks to smash them and the bone marrow is then consumed. Small birds' eggs may be broken in the same manner whereas larger ostrich eggs are cracked by throwing stones at them.

Man's rubbish can also provide vultures with a varied menu. They will swoop into urban areas and collect tasty trash. They provide a refuse service in these regions, removing both natural and manmade rubbish and, unlike lots of other scavengers, are well-tolerated as a result . . . waste not, want not.

# WHY DO OCTOPUSES HAVE BEAKS?

An octopus spends a lot of its time sitting in its den looking out. Inquisitive by nature, it is always on the alert for something new. When its curiosity is aroused, the head pokes up for a better view of what's happening. It has great eyesight. When out browsing an octopus feels around everything examining rocks, cracks and stones. Once dinner is spotted, it attacks. Octopuses sometimes scavenge for bits of dead fish but, not surprisingly, prefer their food live and fresh — crabs, prawns, oysters and sometimes each other! Octopi occasionally make meals of parts of themselves — a practice called AUTOPHAGY — they are not above nibbling on one of their own tentacles when feeling peckish!

After a swift lunge forward its unsuspecting prey becomes trapped in its arms. The octopus then returns home to dine and will often collect other bits of food *en route*, sometimes killing several small animals before settling down to eat one. Once in the grasp of an octopus it is thumbs down for a crab. A hungry octopus secretes a special poison to paralyse its catch. This poison has another important function: it helps predigest the victim before it's finally eaten. The beak or RANULA, similar to a parrot's but blunter, sets to work. This acts as a very versatile tool for the octopus. It can be pushed out of its mouth and then drawn back in, dragging food with it.

One might think that the octopus would eat using its many arms and tentacles, placing food directly into its mouth. This isn't the case. The octopus prefers using its hard brown beak to remove crab meat from the shell. If the octopus manages to get its tentacles around an oyster — no problem. The beak is multi-purpose and can be used as a drill. After a hole is bored through the shell, the paralysing digestive juice is squirted in and the octopus simply sucks its gourmet meal out.

The beak of an octopus can also be used for defence and humans sometimes fall victim to its bite. A bit like a bee sting, some bites produce more serious symptoms, especially if the victim is allergic. At the time of the bite you generally feel no pain. They rarely break the skin and only if their poisonous saliva is injected will there be discomfort. Don't worry — much as they may try to paralyse and predigest you, they would never manage to eat you!

# WHY DO SQUIRRELS
## HAVE SUCH BIG TAILS?

Dragging a huge tail around all day long, up trees and over walls can't be easy for a squirrel. So, what's the pay-off? It obviously helps make them look cute, but having a tail that accounts for half its size must do more. These ingenious little creatures have worked out how to get maximum benefit from their cumbersome tails.

A squirrel's tail can lend itself to almost anything. In winter, the tail acts as an overcoat. It fluffs up and wraps around the little furry body, helping the squirrel brave harsh weather conditions. As the seasons change so, too, does the role of the tail which becomes a portable sunshade at the height of summer. When the sun is shining, the squirrel sits in the shadow of its own tail. If they want to sunbathe, squirrels simply lie on a branch letting their tails flop down.

As squirrels don't hang out in flocks or herds, they often use their tails to flash signals to their forest neighbours. "Tail language" is known by every squirrel. Fluffing, waving and flicking are all part of this rodent's complex communication system.

It is well known that squirrels are sprightly and nimble. If they manage to keep standing still for a minute, the tail points skywards. It behaves like a rudder when its owner is running and stretches out behind when leaping. It is almost as if the tail shifts into different gears depending on the squirrel's actions.

Squirrels definitely make the most of what nature has given them. The tail is truly this agile rodent's best friend!

# WHEN DO FISH GROWL?

When they are going through an identity crisis . . .

No, seriously, fish have indeed been known to let out the odd growl and can join in the general clamour of the sea with different sound-producing devices.

The ability to make noise implies that fish have ears to hear all this rumpus – and they do! Some even have organs to amplify the sounds they hear and what other fish are saying. Having the **SWIM BLADDER** attached to their ears helps them detect lots of marine noises. Other fish actually produce sounds by vibrating their swim bladder with special muscles. Male fish often growl before attacking an intruder in their territory. If this threat or warning is ignored, fighting can occur, however, in silence.

Females often become vocal after spawning and again when caring for their brood. Angelfish, when disturbed or bothered by something, emit high-pitched sounds to express their annoyance. Clownfish have quite

a well-developed communication system using many different sounds. Purring, not growling, often occurs in courtship. Males have a marked effect on females when they woo them with their marine music. But if the female isn't interested she will squawk back at him to forget it.

So, how are fish able to make all these sounds? They don't have a voicebox and therefore must rely on other methods. Haddock, for instance, croak using the swimbladder. Air is circulated around it using external muscles. Other fish grind their teeth to produce threatening sounds to ward off uninvited visitors and to deter rivals and intruders. If fish can growl and make many other noises and hear the sounds of their mates, can they be trained to respond to man?

Yes, but they won't react unless there is something in it for them, namely food. As with birdsong, fish can growl, squeak, drone, squawk, croak and purr. With today's technological advances, perhaps it's only a matter of time before we discover the dawn chorus of the deep!

# How Are Foxes Like Cats?

Foxes belong to the same family as dogs; both are **CANIDS**. Obviously, they share lots of traits with some other canines – long muzzles, pointed erect ears, intelligence. Interestingly enough though, foxes also closely resemble cats.

Felines are famous for their agility and balance. Foxes share this sense of balance and co-ordination. They are able to run along the narrowest walls and fences with little difficulty. Having retractable claws like a cat's helps them climb large trees, often without the aid of low-growing branches.

Dogs and other members of the canid group have strong pack instincts, preferring to hunt in groups. Foxes don't share this behaviour. Like cats, they are solitary hunters. Probably just as well, as a rabbit wouldn't go very far in feeding a group of hungry foxes. The victims of a fox's predatory nature are usually rodents and birds. When young and learning to hunt, most foxes develop a catlike pounce. Prey are often caught after a swift leap. The fox springs into the air, aided by its long hind legs, and then dives directly on to its dinner. This is exactly what cats do to prevent their prey from escaping. This strange similarity even extends to both animals flicking their tails just prior to pouncing. Birds are also caught in this foxy feline fashion.

Because most of their hunting is done at night, seeing in the dark is a must. In daylight the pupil becomes a vertical slit similar to a cat's eyes. At night it gets much bigger, helping the fox to see better. "Cats' eyes," both on cats and the manmade kind in the middle of the road, reflect a car's headlights. Foxes' eyes do too.

Having whiskers or VIBRISSAE is not unique to foxes and cats. Lots of animals have these special sensory hairs, but the whiskers on a fox are different from whiskers on other canids. Growing quite long, often over ten centimetres on each side of their nose, their whisker span is often wider than the widest part of their body. This is important when crawling through undergrowth and for accurately landing on prey.

What is it with foxes? Isn't it great that a member of the dog family behaves like a member of the cat family? Well, learning that adaptability is the name of the game has ensured their success worldwide.

# Why Do Birds Of A
# Feather Flock Together?

Everyone has seen hundreds of noisy starlings flying and landing in huge groups. How come they never seem to bump into each other? Is there a leader bird? Why do they congregate in such huge numbers? Well, as with shoaling in fish, flocking decreases the risk of a single bird being attacked. It improves the chances of an individual bird being alerted to danger. A bird on its own frequently has to stop feeding in order to scan its surroundings for predators but, if it is a member of a flock, it can spend more time feeding because there will always be a few flock members alert to give the alarm.

The same eyes which keep watch for predators also help in the search for food. Because birds are social creatures, they look out for each other as well. When one bird in the flock finds food, all the other birds in the group come over to investigate. Birds keep an eye on each other even in flight. They learn not to bump into each other, using the same principle as the Mexican wave: each bird will do exactly what the bird on its immediate right is doing. Sticking together when flying is aided by FLOCK MARKERS or white markings on the wings and tail which birds will flash to signal each other. Special FLIGHT CALLS also help to keep the flock intact. Relationships in the flock vary from complete anonymity to total recognition of each other and each bird's status. In big flocks of starlings, the birds really can't decide whether they like or dislike each other. Attracted to each other, they form a flock but they also want to keep their distance so that each bird has sufficient room to feed and fly without hindrance.

In an established flock, individual birds get to know each other and recognise each other's social status so a pecking order develops. Such hierarchies help keep stability and peace in the flock. Communal living suits many species of bird which have learned to recognise that there is, indeed, safety in numbers!

# Why Is A Seahorse Father Also A Mother?

It may sound strange but this is exactly what occurs with these peculiar fish. Their shape alone sets them apart from other fish in that they have necks. Unlike most fish, who swim horizontally, sea horses swim vertically. The breeding habits of this unique fish are totally way-out . . .

Unlike lots of other fish who just lay and leave their eggs, seahorses show an unusually high level of parental care to their offspring. Peculiarly, it is the males not the females of the species that are preoccupied with pregnancy.

When courting, the female seahorse does all the chasing. Her coloration is brighter than the male's. She swims up to him, shows herself and beckons him to follow her. When they've decided to become a couple the female lays her eggs into a little pouch on the male's belly. He then becomes pregnant. This little pocket or **BROOD POUCH** is where the babies develop. The belly skin forms a type of placenta which nourishes the young inside providing them with oxygen.

You may well ask, why doesn't the female sea horse have her own brood pouch? These pouches only develop in the presence of the male hormone **TESTOSTERONE**. The pregnancy or **GESTATION** period is about three weeks long. Every day during this period the female comes over and greets the male who hangs out in the same place for the duration of his pregnancy. Seahorses use their tails to hang on to weeds and rocks. Because they are frequently eaten by crabs, they disguise themselves to resemble reeds and weeds and in so doing have developed very interesting types of skin with various outgrowths and dangly bits in different colours. When the time is up, clouds of tiny seahorses are squirted out from their father's belly – his parental duties complete.

Seahorses do not mate for life. In the event that the father seahorse gets eaten or dies, the roles are reversed with the surviving female looking after the young until she chances upon an unattached male whom she likes. A surviving male will start roaming, looking for a new female, once his pouch is emptied. This type of parental role reversal works so well for seahorses, perhaps we humans should give it a whirl!

# Why Do Lizards Lose Their Tails?

Humans are incapable of regrowing lost appendages, but reptiles – especially lizards – have great powers of regeneration and can literally regrow lost bits of their bodies or tail. But only once because a predator will generally approach its prey from behind, the rear or tail end of a lizard is often the object of attention when this reptile is being stalked. If the predator manages to catch hold of the lizard's tail, it will cleanly break off, continuing to wriggle while the rest of the lizard runs away tail-less. Called **AUTONOMY** or "self-amputation", this process is an example of an animal losing its tail to save its head!

Fortunately for the poor lizard, because of autonomy it will survive. Brute force isn't necessary in making the tail come away. Special break points or lines of weakness are built into the tail. Muscles on either side of the tail contract and the tail parts company with the body. How does the lizard not bleed to death after losing its tail? A thin skin or membrane which runs across the weak point seals off all the blood-vessels and nerves.

Lizards need their tails every day of their lives for balance, running, climbing, courtship and display, so a new tail is grown again quite quickly. But this replacement can't snap off and save the lizard's life a second time. The new tail is just a rod of cartilage and only helps with balance and movement. If a predator manages to grab hold of it, the lizard won't live to tell the tale . . .

# Why Do Bees Swarm?

*"A swarm of bees in May
is worth a load of hay . . .
A swarm of bees in June
is worth a silver spoon . . .
A swarm of bees in July
isn't worth a fly."*

This old farmers' rhyme is very true. The earlier the bees swarm in summer, the better for the bees . . . and the beekeeper. Swarming is natural and usually occurs when a colony of bees decides to split up into two parts. This happens every three years or so — especially if the colony has too many bees in it, or too much honey has been produced. It also happens when a new Queen decides it's time for the old Queen to pack her bags.

The swarm itself consists of the old Queen and about one-third of the workers, or drones, and other bees. Usually the Queen Bee is too heavy to fly, and so for a week beforehand she ceases to lay eggs and goes on a strict diet. All the bees then fly off in a well-formed group. The Queen doesn't lead the swarm, but behaves as if she is just one of the crowd. Sometimes she may get lost and when this happens all the other bees panic and fly back to the mother colony. If all goes well, the swarm soon rests on a tree and may stay there for a couple of days in a massive cluster. This consists of an outer layer or shell of bees around a loosely-packed interior where the Queen is hidden. There is an entrance hole through which the inside of the cluster can be seen. These settled swarms are often attractive to other bees who may join the group from nearby colonies. All the bees in the cluster are tranquil and remain like this for a period of time.

Then scout bees start looking around for a new place to live. When a suitable site has been found, the scout bees guide the swarm to it. As soon as the new nest site is occupied, the bees mate, secrete beeswax and build combs. The Queen starts to gain weight and begins laying again. The workers start gathering pollen and nectar so that enough honey will be produced to last the winter. By the following summer, if all goes well, the whole cycle begins again.

# How Do Sharks Bite?

Sharks are unique in animal evolution. They have stayed the same since their appearance over 300 million years ago. It is as if chance had made them perfectly adapted to their environment from the start. They live in all the seas from the Arctic to the Atlantic and range in length from twenty inches to seventy feet.

Nature would find it difficult to improve on the superb design of the shark's mouth. No terrestrial predator comes anywhere near matching the perfection of the shark's jaws, which have evolved from the skeleton of the gills. Unlike man, the shark's upper jaw can separate or disengage from the skull providing this ocean stalker with two mobile and independent jaws. This enables it to swallow prey much larger than itself and tear off enormous pieces of flesh. Feeding on large fish or marine mammals involves tearing off whole mouthfuls of flesh. Some can remove lumps up to 20 kg with one bite!

The spectacular distance these jaws can

open would be nothing were they not supported by muscles of exceptional power facilitating the shark's vice-like grip. Housed inside this cavernous mouth are rows and rows of razor-sharp saw-edged teeth which are replaced as they are lost or broken. These are derived from its fish-scales. When the jaws separate before an attack these spiky molars point forwards and outwards, thus enabling this voracious fish to dig in and grab hold of its prey. The wounds left by the formidable jaw of the great white shark can be dramatic and horrendous. This is one cookie that definitely doesn't nibble! Not all sharks, however, are killers. Some are scavengers and the largest sharks, such as the basking shark and the white shark, just eat plankton.

Unlike other marine animals which have won our sympathy and have become the focus of conservation movements, sharks are still numbered among the most feared creatures of the sea. This doesn't entitle us to eradicate them. It is up to us to adapt ourselves to the shark — not the other way around!

# Why Do Cats Like Catnip?

They smell it, they chew it, they eat it, and then they behave in the most bizarre fashion imaginable. Maybe catnip shouldn't be legal for cats at all!

What is it anyway? Catnip or "Catmint" is a fuzzy, fragrant plant with blue flowers. Its official name is **NEPETA CATARIA**. Cats just adore it and may get "high" by chewing or eating it. They enjoy soft toys much more if stuffed with catnip. It is even possible to get aerosol cans filled with catnip scent to spray on toys for your cat's pleasure!

After sniffing, eating, or sucking on toys filled with this plant, female cats will often behave as if in heat. It was once thought that the plant actually caused them to come into season. We now know that this is not true because it affects male and female cats in the same way and male cats don't even come into season. The question remains how and why does catnip affect cats? Why don't all cats roll over and stare into space after ingesting it? Well, it's a distant relative of a psychedelic drug and cats may get high by chewing or eating it.

The urine of the tomcat often causes female cats in heat to roll over and behave strangely. It can cause funny behaviour in toms too. Perhaps there is some substance in catnip which resembles the urine of the tom and drives other cats wild. Perhaps not; it may just be that cats simply enjoy the "catnip sensation" and it's probably totally unrelated to sex, drugs or tomcats' pee. Maybe that's enough said on the matter.

# How Do Spiders Hunt?

Most spiders are carnivorous. In addition to silk glands they have venom glands as well. Most use this venom to kill their prey but only a few species are strong enough or have fangs long enough to penetrate a victim. The Black Widow is the most notorious and deadly of all venom-producing spiders. Others rely on disguising and concealing themselves using webs and the like. We all know how a web works – an unfortunate fly becomes entangled in its sticky threads and struggles to release itself. It usually fails. The spider sits in ambush with its front legs stretched out to pick up vibrations from the web. When it senses that dinner has just landed, it rushes out to the fly, wraps it up in sticky threads and then bites it. Fangs pierce the prey, injecting venom. The venom paralyses the prey and digestive juices are then squirted into the immobilised insect turning its insides into a liquid meal. The spider proceeds to suck this concoction up into its stomach.

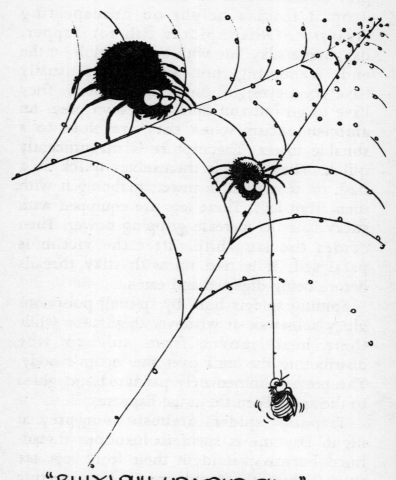

..."BILLY! PULL UP YOUR FLY..."

Net-casting spiders don't sit and wait for prey to come to them. They weave a net and drop it from a height on unsuspecting creatures. Other spiders fish for supper, dangling a silky line with a sticky glob on the end. Wandering, non-web spiders usually have good eyesight, unlike web spiders. They have to go out and catch their own prey. An ambush occurs when they are close to a suitable insect. The capture is magnificently quick. They launch themselves quick as a flash on to a suitable insect, grabbing it with their front legs. These legs are equipped with sticky hairs to increase gripping power. Then comes the fang-bite. After the victim is paralysed, it is tied up with silky threads before being digested and eaten.

Spitting spiders hunt by spitting poisonous gluey substance at whatever they fancy while their head moves from side to side distributing the stuff over the victim's body. The prey is immediately paralysed and glued to the spot. Then the usual happens . . .

Trapdoor spiders ambush their prey at night. Daytime is spent in luxurious thread-lined burrows; at night their front legs are stuck out of the trapdoor. An unsuspecting insect out for a stroll walks too close to the burrow and — wham! — it will never walk again.

The tarantula's hunting method of ambush is quite heroic. Tarantulas climb trees and peer down, waiting for "tea" to pass by underneath. Then they jump down on to their prey and ram their ice-pick fangs into the victim's body. Luckily for us, tarantulas don't view humans as "tea." Preferring not to eat out, all their food is eaten at home.

The water spider is the only ARACHNID that lives underwater. These spiders don't build webs, preferring to hunt while wandering around freely. They swim about, attacking small flies and crustaceans which they bring back to their air bubble to be eaten. Water spiders usually attach their air bubble homes to plants. Because they breathe air just like land spiders, they must take a supply of it below the surface. They travel around underwater with their abdomen stuck to an air bubble. Unlike us, spiders don't breathe through their mouths but through SPIRACLES in their abdomens instead.

As you can well imagine, the predatory hunting nature of spiders curtails their social encounters with other spiders. When courting, the male has to be very clever not to become both mate and meal for the female spider!

# What Is In a Camel's Hump?

The one-humped Arabian camel and two-humped Bactrian are the only domesticated members of the whole camel family. They got their humps as a result of living in dry arid places.

Not all humps are created equally. Shape and size vary from animal to animal. A Bactrian's humps are inclined to flop over sideways, especially as the animal gets old. The Arabian's just shrinks in size. These changes are natural signs of ageing. Because of where they live, these large mammals need lots of water – they can drink about 140 litres at a time. This keeps them going for quite a while because they produce very little urine. Even though they can drink up to one-third of their body weight in water, it is neither stored in the humps nor in the stomach but is distributed throughout the blood and tissue of the body as it is in all mammals.

Fat in most mammals is usually dispersed and stored throughout the body. Not in Bactrians and Arabians. Most of their fat is stored in the hump. This is a special adaptation to help the camel keep from overheating. If this fat were dispersed under the skin all over the body it would act like a thick blanket insulating an already very warm animal. Because nearly all the fat is kept in the one place, camel meat is remarkably fat-free. Hump size on male animals increases greatly after they have been castrated due to changes in their metabolism. The skin over the hump is very elastic and expands as the hump grows. Farm camels are frequently castrated so that their humps will grow — camel fat is a highly-prized delicacy.

The hump isn't just a huge fatty deposit perched on the camel's back. It is composed of fat all right, but a special elastic tissue surrounds it keeping it in place, attaching it to the camel's spine. The hump is also richly supplied with blood. It is important for working camels that the hump doesn't get too big because it becomes difficult to fit a camel saddle.

This chubby lump is obviously an important feature for the camel and at certain times of year it comes in quite handy for camel-handlers too. During the breeding season the males urinate and defecate with increased frequency. The camel's tail is used to flick this waste so that it sprays everywhere. The solution to this is to tie the tail up to the long hair on the hump; this helps everyone keep clean!

# WHY DO ELEPHANTS HAVE TRUNKS?

They say elephants never forget and that they are afraid of mice, but it is the appearance of these strange-looking creatures, with their thin tails and long trunks that raises most comment. This trunk is not merely a cosmetic touch but a superb piece of design by Mother Nature well worth its strange appearance.

Anatomically the trunk is both the elephant's nose and upper lip, with nostrils running through its entire length. Made up of muscle and very flexible, the trunk is effectively a fifth limb. So, what does this odd arm attached to the elephant's face allow it to do? For a start, it comes in handy during courtship allowing the Romeo elephant to caress the loved one. Elephants frequently put their trunks into each other's mouths as a sign of affection or to swap information.

On a more practical level, it is an invaluable "comfort tool" allowing the elephant to rub itchy skin! When the elephant is neither loving nor rubbing, it is feeding or exploring. The trunk is used to put food into

its mouth. Elephant calves learn to eat by sampling food items in mother's mouth. While the nostrils are generally used for breathing, the elephant's ability to nose-drink is unique among mammals. They can also suck up mud or dust to squirt all over themselves or over another elephant if the mood so takes them.

The trunk has another more serious function — detection! As an exploratory organ, it provides much of the elephant's information on its environment. At the first sign of danger, the trunk is raised aloft to locate the scent. It is not, however, used for fighting, as damage, however slight, can greatly diminish the elephant's chances of survival. If irritated, an elephant will lash out its trunk at whatever is hassling it, but it is not used in an attack. When charging, the elephant carries the trunk limply and attacks using its tusks. Rather like a rather rotund submarine, the trunk is the elephant's periscope, while the tusks are the torpedoes used in battle.

# Why Do Owls Have
# Such Round Faces?

An owl perching on a branch often appears to be top-heavy. The head is large and round, resting on a little body; the face is characteristically saucer-shaped. The eyes, which resemble those of many deep-sea fish are relatively larger than those of other birds and occupy a lot of the front of the owl's skull. Like our own eyes, the owl's face forward, enabling the owl, like us, to have binocular or stereoscopic vision. However, unlike our moveable eyes, the circular eyes of this nocturnal hunter are fixed in their sockets. So, to see sideways with both eyes it must rotate its extremely mobile neck around to the side. The circle of feathers or FILOPLUMES that surround the eyes on the owl's face also add to its rounded features. These feathery circles are used in the same way that other animals use their large fleshy ears — as funnels for conducting and concentrating sound to the ears. An owl doesn't hear using the filoplumes. It hears with its small ears – the filoplumes just direct and amplify the sounds it hears. The filoplumes around the left eye are directed downwards while those surrounding the right eye face upwards. The owl moves its head up and down to help pinpoint where its next meal is hiding.

The owl's ears themselves, which are just big holes, are placed unevenly or asymmetrically on either side of the head. They are highly sensitive and can catch the sound of a mouse squeaking and certain other high-pitched sounds produced by a rodent's movement through grass. These sounds help the owl establish not only the presence of prey, but also its exact location in partial or complete darkness. Its acute sense of hearing is further enhanced by the ears being placed so far apart.

So you can see that the organs of seeing and hearing are vitally important to the owl, and therefore a large skull is needed to house them. The visual and audial organs fill the owl's large head which is so perceptive that it resembles a mini mobile radio scanner! Hearing and seeing are fundamental to an owl's hunting technique. This explains why their ears and eyes are so big and accounts for why owls have such big, round faces.

# WHY DO HIPPOS WALLOW IN WATER?

Mud, mud, glorious mud – do hippos wallow to cool their blood? Well, sort of . . . the hippopotamus or "river horse" is very much at home in water. Resting on top of a barrel-shaped torso and stumpy legs is the hippo's enormous head. Positioned on top of the head are slit-like nostrils which can be sealed off when submerged. Periscope eyes enable observation just above the surface of the water. Hippos can remain completely submerged for up to five minutes. Then the whole broad square muzzle is raised and water is blown noisily from the nostrils.

A hippo's days are spent doing just this. They only come on to dry land at night and spend about six hours every evening feeding. Because so much of their time is spent just wallowing they need relatively little food compared with other hoofed mammals. Their energy requirements for muscle tone are also reduced because they spend so much time resting in warm water.

Hippos have terribly thick skin, but the outer layer is very thin. This thin surface skin seems to act like a wick. It allows water to pass through it in both directions. So, in dry weather water loss through the skin is great — much higher than in other mammals. Hippos, however, have it sussed. To keep from becoming dehydrated they just hang out in water all day. Their thick skin has very few sweat glands so, unlike humans, they can't sweat to cool down. Instead, they have special glands which produce a pink substance resembling sticky sweat. This substance actually acts as a high-protection factor sun-cream, helping to protect the skin against ultraviolet rays. The mud in which they liberally cover themselves also helps prevent sunburn and protects them from biting flies. While hippos seem to escape the attentions of ticks and other pests which irritate most land-dwelling animals they are, unfortunately, beset by leeches instead.

Because they are in water most of the time, this is where lots of fighting occurs. The males are very violent and often slash each other with their huge teeth. After a fight, the loser lowers its head in defeat while the victor parades around threateningly with its mouth wide open until the defeated hippo disappears. Mating, too, happens whilst wallowing, and birth often occurs in water. Young hippos sometimes even suckle while submerged. Luckily for other hippos close by, they do manage to make it on to dry land for one thing — their enormous poos.

# How Do Fish Sleep?

Because they've got no eyelids, fish can't close their eyes. Yet they need regular sleep just like you and I. Adopting unexpected positions and postures at night, some lie on their sides, while others float with their tails pointing straight up towards the water's surface. After swimming around in shoals all day, they each go to their own sleeping quarters on the seabed, all pointing in different directions. If disturbed, they immediately wake up and form the shoal again. Many actually lie on their sides when they want to sleep. You'd think that flatfish, which live on the seabed, could just stop wherever they are and snooze. This is not the case at all. At night, young sole swim to the surface and, turning their body into a saucer shape, sleep. Plaice simply float a few inches up from the seabed before sleeping, somewhat like you hovering above the mattress! Others, like the parrot fish, kip in a sleeping-bag which it makes each evening out of slime and bubbles. A sleeping fish can

" HE SAID HE WAS GOING TO SLEEP....BUT
I'M NOT CONVINCED..."

sometimes be handled and even lifted out of the water before they begin to struggle free. Some fish change colour when asleep, perhaps to aid disguise. Those that spend the day amongst the coral go to underwater caves at night.

One would expect that fish, if they yawned at all, would do so each evening when they're tired like we do, and again in the morning upon waking. Yawning is important because during sleep the blood flow slows down and blood becomes sluggish and clogged with carbon dioxide. The morning yawn takes in fresh oxygen and sets the blood coursing again. But fish are funny; they yawn at midday when they've been active. If a fish has been lazy it will yawn to liven itself up and generate some energy before moving off. Excitement or danger will also cause fish to yawn, toning up their muscles for a quick escape.

So, you know what they say, "let sleeping dogs lie . . . " Why not do the same for sleeping fish?

## IF YOU WOULD LIKE TO KNOW:

- How salmon find their way home
- Why hens dustbathe
- How insects breathe
- How to tell the age of a whale
- Why birds have grit inside them
- Why some animals have hooves while others have claws
- How animals get their vitamins
- How the mouths of carnivores and herbivores differ?

. . . then pick up a copy of *Andrew's Animals* II — out soon!